Anonymous

Good Roads

Anonymous

Good Roads

ISBN/EAN: 9783744731829

Printed in Europe, USA, Canada, Australia, Japan

Cover: Foto ©Thomas Meinert / pixelio.de

More available books at **www.hansebooks.com**

NEW MAIL

Cushion Tires.   .... $100.

Tangent Spokes.

Drop Forgings Throughout.

New Mail, Special Pattern,—Low Handle Bars.

All Parts Strictly Interchangeable.

Handsomest Wheel Made.

ALSO $135 GRADE.   ALSO $100 LADY'S PATTERN.
  "   35 BOYS.   "   PNEUMATIC NEW MAILS.

New Mail High Grade, Light Weight "Scorcher"
with Pneumatic Tires, '92 Model, out in March.

... SEND FOR CATALOGUE ...

MANUFACTURERS:

WM. READ & SONS,

107 WASHINGTON ST.,   BOSTON, MASS.

WESTERN WHEEL WORKS

Samples of 1892 Wheels Ready for Inspection.

THEY CONSIST OF TWELVE DIFFERENT PATTERNS, AND RANGE IN PRICE
FROM $25.00 TO $135.00, FITTED WITH CUSHION
AND PNEUMATIC TIRES.

IT IS THE MOST COMPLETE LINE EVER OFFERED TO THE TRADE.

Examine our goods and get prices before placing your orders ..... Send for Catalogue.

R. L. COLEMAN & CO.

AGENTS FOR EASTERN, MIDDLE AND SOUTHERN STATES.

35 BARCLAY STREET AND 40 PARK PLACE, NEW YORK.

GOOD ROADS.

Plan and Scope.

Each monthly number of **Good Roads** will be illustrated by pictures carefully prepared to accompany the text and designed to illustrate with special force the value of

Better Roads and Better Streets.

The general aim of this magazine will be to stimulate the interest of the public concerning the advantages of good roads and streets, and the best **methods of constructing and maintaining them.** In pursuance of this object we shall publish from time to time the

Best Articles Obtainable

relating not only to the economic features of the movement, but showing also by both text and illustration, the MOST APPROVED METHODS of improving the public streets and roads.

The extended favor and largely increased demand with which the recently published pamphlet, "The Gospel of Good Roads" has been received, will more than justify us in reproducing it in the first numbers of our magazine. Other articles of value are now in hand and will follow in due order.

Special Features.

We intend to make this magazine of interest and value to every person who travels the common roads, to every driver of horses and to every user of wheeled vehicles. Special attention will be given to the subject of

Road Laws and Legislation,

including outlines of existing laws and suggestions for local and general acts looking to the better making and maintaining of public highways.

Country Roads.

Under this heading will be included much practical information of special value to the suburban resident, the farmer and other persons whose homes and places of business are so located, as to compel them to make frequent use of the dirt wagon roads which are found so commonly in all parts of the country.

Town and Village Streets.

These subjects will receive thorough and practical treatment, and extended information will be published from time to time, showing costs and methods of improvement, including plans and specifications of approved merit.

During the coming Winter we shall devote considerable space in our columns to the description of various kinds of machinery and implements used in making and repairing roads, with impartial comment upon the relative values of machine and hand work in the various departments of road making and maintenance. Information will be given relative to the cost, value, durability and uses of road rollers, stone and rock crushers, scrappers, hones, etc., etc., and correspondence will be invited upon all these subjects.

although all matter tending to advertise the qualities of any particular article of manufacture will be excluded from our reading column.

Wheeled Vehicles.

It is our intention to publish articles of special value to the makers and users of **wagons, carriages and all kinds of wheeled vehicles,** showing practical methods and compiling valuable hints relating to the use and care of these vehicles, and the relation which they bear, in their economy and use, to the streets and highways upon which they are employed.

Every Rider and Driver should Read "Good Roads."

Permanent Departments.

These will include, as among the most important :

1. Popular Opinion.

Under this heading we shall publish the expressions of our best citizens, and more important exchanges concerning the movement for better roads.

2. News and Comment.

Will include a full and careful record of the progress of roads and street improvement wherever such work may be carried on.

3. Queries and Answers.

This most important department will be devoted to the publishing and answering of such questions as may be asked by correspondents, upon any subject properly within the scope of our work, and such questions will receive the fullest and most careful attention.

To Summarize.

It is our intention to make GOOD ROADS **the most valuable and complete compendium of road improvement litera-**

ture ever published. The subscription price ($2.00 per annum) places it easily within the reach of every mature reader, while its value as an advertising medium is evidenced by the fact that **we begin publication with an assured list of more than 23,000 paid subscribers.**

Good Roads

will publish during the coming year a list of SERIAL ARTICLES on LEADING SUBJECTS pertaining to the improvement of ROADS and STREETS. These articles will include among others, the following :

The Gospel of Good Roads,

being a reprint of this popular illustrated "Letter to the American Farmer," for which a wide demand has been created.

Macadam and Telford Roads.

A thoroughly practical, illustrated treatise on all the details of road making and maintenance according to the systems of Macadam and Telford, together with extended reference to kindred methods.

Dirt Roads and Gravel Roads.

Showing how they should be **made, drained** and **repaired ;** the relative values of road materials ; grades ; locating and **alignment ; system of repairs,** etc., etc.

Street Pavements.

A fully illustrated article on the important subject of **pavements for town and village streets** will form a leading feature in several successive numbers of **Good Roads.** This article will treat of the historical and descriptive side of the pavement subject, as well as the **practical methods of paving ;** relative values as viewed from various standpoints, durability, cost, tractive qualities, etc., etc.

Other Serial Articles will be Announced in Due Season.

A Squirrel needs no

science to teach him how to get the meat out of the nut. But it needs a lot of science to teach a man how to get a *digestible* and *delicious* drink out of the cocoa bean. Van Houten & Zoon have solved this great problem. Not only is the excess of fat removed, effecting a gain of **one-third** in strength, but by a Secret Process they increase the *solubility* of the flesh-forming elements by **50 per cent.**, *bring out* the flavor and aroma, and produce a superb beverage, which is certified as *pure, easily digested* and *nutritious*, by the highest analysts in Europe.

VAN HOUTEN'S
COCOA,
PERFECTLY PURE.

"Best & Goes Farthest."

CAP'EN CUTTLE.

A comparison will quickly prove the great superiority of VAN HOUTEN'S COCOA. *Take no substitute.* Sold in 1-8, 1-4, 1-2 and 1 lb. Cans. ☞ If not obtainable, enclose 25 cts. to either VAN HOUTEN & ZOON, 106 Reade Street, New York, or 45 Wabash Ave., Chicago, and a can, containing sufficient for 35 to 40 cups, will be mailed to address given. *Mention this publication.* Prepared only by the *inventors*, VAN HOUTEN & ZOON, Weesp, Holland.   c 5.

"Cap'en Cuttle knows a good thing, I tell ye; and when he hails a better drink than Van Houten's Cocoa he'll make a note on it."

Shall you ride a Bicycle next
year?

Do you want to ride the
best?

One built in the best equipped Bicycle factory in
the world?

We suggest that you have
a good look at the Victors'
for '92.

They will lead next year as
they have in the past.

OVERMAN WHEEL CO
BOSTON,
WASHINGTON,
SAN FRANCISCO,
DENVER.

Good Roads.

Vol. I.   JANUARY, 1892.   No. I.

THE GOSPEL OF GOOD ROADS.

BY ISAAC B. POTTER.

A COUNTY ROAD IN JERSEY.

INTRODUCTION.

HAVE heard of a very clever woman whose otherwise excellent husband disturbed the felicity of the household about
twice in each year by making himself very drunk. The good
wife, despairing of the common and commonly hopeless remedy
of moral suasion, applied her wits to the discovery of a newer
and more effective means of appealing from Philip drunk to Philip sober.
On the occasion of his next debauch, when he was brought home in a condition of maudlin helplessness, with clothing smeared and torn, eyes bleared
and face inflamed by drink, she sent for the photographer and caused a life-
size picture of her limp lord to be taken, which was duly finished in appropriate colors, framed and hung in a place of honor in the family reception
room, where she insisted upon keeping it for a period of three months, and

made known her vow to double the term whenever the offense should be
repeated. That picture was a silent and successful preacher.

It has seemed to me that if national errors could be reflected in the same
forcible way ; if some power could and would

> "the giftie gie us.
> to see ourselves as others see us."

we should get to the end of many of our difficulties. The dirt roads of
America are heavy drinkers. They lead a staggering and uncertain course
from town to town ; smear themselves with thick mire ; for four months in
the year are unfit for the company of respectable people, and less than
eighteen months ago got themselves regularly indicted by the grand jury.*
The pictures of roads shown in the following article are made from photo-
graphs. Like all truthful pictures they are better than words, and if they
shall supply force to the imperfect work which I have put together in the
odd moments picked from the hours of an exacting profession, I shall feel
that I am doubly paid for my trouble, that the pictures themselves are a
sufficient reason for their existence, and shall owe an abundant gratitude to
the friends by whose aid they have been obtained.   I. B. P.

I.

To the American Farmer:

In these days, when the voice of your complaint is loud in
the land, and a thousand partisans are declaiming a thousand
theories to account for the "decline of agriculture," I will try to
write you a letter, in which, I believe, I can make it appear that
the greatest remedy for the cure of unprofitable farming lies in
your own hands.

It is a thankless, unpopular, and, in some respects, a dis-
couraging thing to preach reform, and the man who undertakes
it for your benefit is entitled to your everlasting regard. I am
going to make that claim upon you, and you will be more ready
to square the account when you know that I am opposed to high
taxes, and to the placing of undue burdens upon the farmer, and
that I am only trying to show you a way for the enrichment of
your slender purse and the betterment of your condition.

The man who lives on a farm should be happier for every
association of farm life. It is a splendid thing to breathe pure
air, drink pure water and have a hundred acres of elbow-room.

---

* On January 14, 1880, the grand jury of Union County, N. J., came into court with a
formal presentment against the old roads ; declaring that "public interests demand that these
roads be repaired and put in good condition at once."

Another thing, every farming community is a community of homes. You have something to be proud of in that. It broadens your manhood and makes you know you have a sacred spot to love and defend. It makes you a good citizen, and a tender husband and father. I wouldn't give much for the patriotism of a man whose only interest in the nation can be packed in a carpet bag. He is not the man for the times when his country is in peril, and when the air trembles with the noise of battle you will find the great bulwark of defense to be made up of volunteers from the farms and firesides. Most great men have been born in the country, and no child of genius ever yet thrived in a boarding-house. The great and successful government is always a government of homes.

And I want to acknowledge the importance and grandeur of your vocation. It is the prime source of all national wealth, and, under proper conditions, it should make you the happiest and most independent of mortals. By the fruits of your toil humanity is sustained, and to reward your industry the coffers of the world are open.

But these are the incidents of your calling. Personally you inherit the common foibles of the race, and you are not aloof from the errors nor exempt from the misfortunes which beset us all. In all kindness let me remind you that in other years you and your good neighbors have opposed many great improvements which were intended for our common benefit, and which the lapse of time has placed in the highest niches of human advancement. You do not forget that when the first railroads were projected you appeared before the legislature of your state and opposed the granting of franchises to all such iniquitous schemes. You said that the locomotives would burn your crops and set fire to the wool on the backs of your sheep ; that the gases from the smoke stack would poison your family and your farm stock, and that travel in a railroad car at the frightful speed of twenty miles an hour would be fatal to many passengers and dangerous to all. You opposed the telegraph and ridiculed the mowing machine. You took the sewing machine on sufferance and regarded the patent thresher with a suspicious eye ; and I might almost say there is no great invention of commercial or agricultural value which was cheered at its birth by the warmth of your approval.

It is best that I should remind you of these things. I do it without malice, for I am somewhat of a farmer myself, and in this most friendly communication it is best that we begin with the frank understanding on all sides that, in spite of your great intelligence, events have proven that, like the rest of mankind, you are likely to err. We don't always recognize a good thing at first sight.

You have changed your opinions about many things because you did not at first understand their value. Observation, argument and experience have helped you out of many an error ; and I am sure you will pardon me if I suggest that you have never yet learned the value of a good road ; for upon this subject you have had neither observation nor experience, and without these, argument is certain to go astray. Let me remind you by one or two illustrations taken from your personal history.

The scythe and the flail are no longer the best tools of your trade, and you long since ceased to shoot crows with the old flint-lock. A few years ago one of your venturesome neighbors went to the state fair and brought home a patent reaper. A little later an enterprising drummer sold him a thresher and a fanning mill. He was a brainy neighbor, with plenty of nerve and a confidence in his own judgment, and you profited by his experience. You looked over the fence while he was at work and became satisfied that the old way of doing things involved an extravagant waste of time and labor ; and you soon found that the money spent for farming machinery was well invested. Then they ran a line of railroad up through your county, and after a while you discovered that it was cheaper and vastly quicker to ride on the cars than to go long journeys by the common road ; and you have been on tolerably good terms with that railroad ever since.

Each of these splendid improvements has filled a want. Proving first its usefulness and then its necessity, it has found a market. You cannot half succeed without it. Did you ever think how it was that all these labor-saving things were first brought to your attention ? They were not born in a public institution nor invented by a public officer— not one of them ; they were not put in use by the vote of a town meeting nor by proclamation of the governor ; they are no part of the public business, and in bestowing their benefits they have been careful to avoid the sluggish turn of the public mill. It all came about in quite a different way. Do you remember how you first came to buy a mower? A wide-awake Yankee told you that he had a machine for cutting grass by horse-power ; that this machine would do better and cleaner work than your scythe, and that, too, at the rate of an acre an hour. You said " Nonsense !" He took his mower down into your meadow, and in a good-natured way proved to you that you could save money in buying that machine ; that you had been paying too much for hired help and boarding too many extra hands in harvest time. You bought that mower, and though you paid what seemed a round figure, you now know that it has paid for itself many times over.

And so you see at the outset, that the mower was rather forced upon you, as were the horse-rake and the reaper and all the rest of the splendid things in the category of farming machinery. You have taxed yourself to pay for these improvements. There is no philanthropy in trade, and you have paid cost and profit to the manufacturer till he has grown rich in the business ; but on the other side of the account it appears that the millions of money spent by the farmers of the United States for improved machines have been repaid to them a hundred fold by the saving of time, labor and money which the old methods would have entailed. You have shared benefits and divided profits with the manufacturer, and your money has gone unbewailed to pay for a splendid thing. Your tax has turned out to be an investment, and in the year 1880 you had over four hundred millions of dollars invested in farm implements and machinery.

But I began with the intention of writing to you about roads— the common road that leads from your door-yard to the nearest market. Did it ever occur to you that this road is part of the machinery of agriculture ? That your farm wagon is a machine, pure and simple, and that the road bears the same relation to your wagon that the steel rail bears to the railway car ? It will do you no harm to think of this a moment, and to remember that every great improvement is the child of thought. The head will ever guide the hand, and every splendid thing you ever did was born and bred in your brain. When the people think, the nation moves ; and a government of sluggards is next door to a government of slaves.

If I could be sure that your strong sense would be put to work in the settling of this question of better roads, my letter to you might stop right here ; but I know that your thoughts are every day directed in the channel where flows the tide of your personal affairs, and in these times of fierce competition you have little to give to the settlement of public questions. You have taken things as you have found them, and long use of dirt roads has almost persuaded you that they are good enough. You are a victim of the ensnaring wiles of custom. "Custom," says Montaigne, " is a violent and treacherous school-mistress. She,

by little and little, slyly and unperceived, slips in the foot of her authority : but having, by this gentle and humble beginning, with the aid of time, fixed and established it, she then unmasks a furious and tyrannic countenance, against which we have no more the courage nor the power so much as to lift our eyes."

I have no axe to grind and have nothing to sell you ; but I want you, as an old friend, to give to this question of good roads the same thought that worked your brain when you bought the mower, for I am going to say some surprising things to you about the country roads, and we shall get on immensely better if

we agree about the facts. And I am going to try to steer clear
of theory ; for the road question is far and away the most important one of the American farmer to-day, and when we talk
about roads it is best to bear in mind that one fact is worth a gross
of guesses, and to apply that scriptural rule, which is no less good
in material than in moral things : " Prove all things ; hold fast
that which is good."

II.

You will agree with me that your roads are bad. You may
not know that they are the very worst in the world ; but you
have never seen nor heard of worse ones ; nor, alas, perhaps of
better. You live on the main road in an important county. I
saw you one day last spring trying to drive your best horse
through the pasty depths of that mysterious streak of public
territory, and while the patient beast was pulling the harness in
two, in his efforts to lift you and your scant load on to the little
bridge near the mill, your photograph was taken, and I have had
it copied on page 6 of this magazine.

It is an honest picture—as honest as the sun ; let us sit down
together and look at it. You will notice that your face is turned
the other way, and I promise not to tell anybody who you are ;
for I feel that the day is soon coming when every American
farmer will look upon that picture with some regret, and I have
no desire to humiliate a friend ; besides, it is not your fault alone
that this road is bad, nor is it this road alone that presents a sea
of slush and slime throughout each rainy season.

There were 10,000 farm horses in your county on the day
when this photograph was taken, and for about four weeks all
the county roads had been in just this condition. Teaming was
out of the question ; to haul a load to town was impossible, and
the 10,000 farm horses stood in their stalls " eating their heads
off." At what cost to the farmers ? Assume that the cost of
keeping each horse is twenty-five cents per day, including labor,
food, and all other items, and in half a minute we compute that
it costs $2,500 per day, $17,500 per week, and exactly $70,000 for
the four weeks that these horses have been standing practically
idle. A bad road, you see, is an expensive thing.

It is expensive not alone to the farmers of your county, but to
the farmers of the entire country. The average rain-fall in the

United States is something over 40 inches per year. The dirt road absorbs these 40 odd inches of water, freezes and thaws, dries, pulverizes, changes from paste to powder and back again from powder to paste, and for weeks at a time is practically impassable.   Farm traffic is tied up.   You have produce to sell, purchases to make, grain to grind, timber to haul, bills to collect and obligations to meet, but all these must wait because your only avenue of travel is taking its annual soak.   A dozen times a day you look out of your barn door with the hope of seeing some struggling vagrant of whom you can inquire, " How is the road?"

I do not intend to overdraw the picture, for we have agreed together to stick to facts alone, and so I have traveled many miles and gone to much trouble in order that my letter to you might contain only the truth, and I find the country roads to be even worse than I had supposed them to be: worse than you think them to be.   They are disgracefully bad almost without exception.   One day I said to myself: " Now, there is the great Empire State ; she is out of debt, rich, populous, thriving ; she has 125 people for every square mile of her territory, nearly 200 incorporated cities and villages, and the value of her farm crops last year was about one and one-half times that of all the New England States combined.   I will go up to the capital county of this great State and see what sort of roads New York has provided for her farmers."   So, one day in April a year ago, I went to Albany, and there, almost in the shadow of that magnificent $25,000,000 state house, I found the farmers of Albany County literally struggling in a " slough of despond."   Here is a picture from an actual sketch made at that time.

Another perfectly honest picture; as honest as the sun. How much do you suppose it costs the farmers of Albany County per day to keep the roads in that condition? The Legislature was then in session, making laws " for the better government of the City of New York," " for the expenditure of money in the repair of State canals," " for improvement of navigation in the Hudson River," " for the completion of the State Capitol," " for the maintenance of convicts in the State Prison," and so on, millions for expenses without end, but nothing in behalf of the farmer. I bought an Albany morning newspaper, and found in that a somewhat extended article on the condition of the roads in the State of New York. Let me quote : *

FARMERS BLOCKED OUT   BAD ROADS KEEP RURAL BUSINESS AT A STAND-STILL.—GRAIN FED TO CATTLE WHOLE BECAUSE IT CANNOT BE TAKEN TO THE MILL.

*　　*　　*　　*　　*　　*　　*　　*　　*

Through correspondence from this and vicinity counties it has been learned that the roads have, during months past, been almost impassable. Business has been impeded, farmers unable to forward produce, and trade in general debarred.

*　　*　　*　　*　　*　　*　　*　　*　　*

The roads in the vicinity of Castleton are in such a shape that it is impossible for farmers to get into the village at all, and business is what may be termed at a standstill. Outside the villages the condition of the roads is by far worse than in former years.

BUSINESS AT A STANDSTILL.

On account of the rough ruts and the very muddy condition of the roads near Guilderland Centre, which are in the worst condition known in years, farmers find it extremely difficult to reach the market with their produce, in consequence of which business has, for some time back, been very dull in this section.

Farmers found it uphill work to raise money enough to pay taxes this spring, and some of those in debt cannot pay their yearly interest. Merchants are also hard pressed, and have large accounts on their books, which, although good, cannot be paid until roads are put in condition so farmers can get to market and sell their accumulated produce.

BAD ROADS BEAT THE RECORD.

The roads in East Berne and vicinity are simply indescribable. They are now beginning to mend, but for the past month they have been almost impassable, and for farmers to attempt to carry a load has been entirely out of the question. Nothing but absolute necessity will induce a farmer to go

---

* See Albany *Argus* of April 16, 1890.

to Albany with a load of produce, and then he finds that 600 or 800 pounds make a heavier burden for his team than 2,400 would with the roads in ordinary condition.

The effect tells seriously on our local merchants. The business at the grist mill suffers because farmers, rather than draw their grain to mill through the deep mud, prefer to feed it to their stock whole. The lumber business has been affected to a greater extent than any other. The winter season is the time when farmers draw logs to the saw-mill to have them sawed into fencing material and for repairing their buildings.

This winter they have been waiting for snow and better roads, until the time has arrived when other duties upon the farm require their attention.

THE CAUSE OF THIS TERRIBLE CONDITION

of the roads is easy of explanation. For the past two months there has not been frost enough in the ground to form a bottom, and the constant travel with frequent rains, has worked the roadbed into mortar, and in many places the

RUTS ARE HUB DEEP.

Nothing like it was ever experienced in that vicinity before. There has never been a season on record when the roads have been bad for so long a period as they have the present season.

The roads near Central Bridge have been almost impassable all winter. So much so that trade has been affected to a great extent. Much of the produce that has always been brought here has been sold for less in places near production. For the past three days, however, they have improved.

The roads in the vicinity of Fonda are in an almost impassable condition, and farmers are unable to bring anything to market if they so desire. As a result, business of all kinds is almost at a standstill. The roads were never in a worse condition than now.

The roads in the vicinity of Clarksville are in a better condition just at present than they have been for the last eight or nine months, which is owing to the absence of rain for a week.

The farmers have been compelled, to a certain extent, to keep their produce at home on account of the condition of the roads. Those residing along the New Scotland plank road, or the Bethlehem turnpike, have the advantage of farmers residing elsewhere. They can go to market at anytime, while people in this vicinity are

COMPELLED TO STAY AWAY.

The worst road for the Clarksville farmers is the Delaware turnpike. From the bridge over the Normanskill to the pavement of Delaware avenue, near Bender's brickyard, it has been impassable a number of times. The roads have been worse for the last two years than before, owing to the large amount of rain that has fallen during that time.

The roads in the vicinity of Hartwick Seminary, for the first time in many months, are

ASSUMING A PASSABLE CONDITION.

The past winter, which has been one totally unlike any previous in the memory of the oldest inhabitants, has also been remarkable for the bad condition of roads. In the villages of Milford and Cooperstown the roads in the main streets have been in a terrible condition, and merchants have attributed the depression of business in no small degree to this. With the pleasant weather of the past few days the roads are gradually growing smooth, and, though still having many deep ruts, farmers are traveling much more. Every year the fact is being more clearly shown that some more effective methods must be adopted to secure better roads in our country districts." * *

From twenty-seven of our states came at that time reports which, without exception, described the public roads to be in a condition not unlike those of Albany County. From one of the wealthiest and most populous western states, a state full of resources and endless possibilities for the farmer, came a photograph, taken on an important country road leading into one of the great cities. I might tell you what city it was, but the scene is no worse than could have been found in the suburbs of a hundred other towns at that time, and I have no desire to excite municipal jealousy. Here, on page 12, is the picture. You see the wagon has become hopelessly stuck, and is abandoned by horse and driver. If that horse could talk, what a story we might have! He would tell you a patient tale of pains and trials that you know not of, and assure you that a dirt road in a civilized country is as much out of place as a dirt roof.

III.

And so it was—and so it is, all over the country. Last March the farmers of Chester County, Pennsylvania, were using a six-horse team to draw a single load of hay. On the 21st day of that month one of the "leaders" in that team stumbled and fell in the deep mud and water which covered the road and was drowned before he could be got out. In Montgomery County, Maryland, during the same month, a lady recovered $2,500 damages from the county for personal injuries received by reason of the bad roads. Costs and disbursements swelled the sum to about $4,000. But these are only incidents, and they have no force except as illustrations. The real unmitigated iniquity of a mud road must be seen by a more extended view.

Let us try a few statistics. You hate statistics and so do I. Take them as they go, they are drier than a mouthful of dust, and we both know what that is. But once in a while the Government sends a man round to count things, just to see whether we

are all here and how we are getting on ; very much in the same
way that we count eggs and chickens and measure rye and oats.
We are dealing with a big subject and one which concerns all
the people. Let us look at it from a standpoint where everybody can see the inspiring spectacle. I want you to understand,
if you do not see it already, that a bad road is really the most
expensive thing in your agricultural outfit ; that it is as much

behind the times as the hand-loom and the flail and the sickle ;
that it has no rightful place in the domain of an intelligent
people.

From official government sources I find that the farmers of
this country, in the year 1890, had upon their farms, draft animals as follows :*

	NUMBER.	VALUE.	AVERAGE PRICE.
Horses	14,213,837	$978,516,562	$68 00
Mules	2,331,027	182,394,099	78 00
Oxen, etc.	36,849,024	560,625,137	15 00
Total	53,393,888	$1,721,535,798	

* These figures are taken from official statistics compiled under direction of the United
States Government authorities at Washington.

Now, to simplify matters a little, you see you have nearly $2,000,000,000 invested in motive power of a perishable, uncertain and expensive kind. Busy or idle, these animals must be fed and cared for every day. They are boarders that you can't get rid of when the busy season is over, and it stands you in hand to keep them at work. Two thousand millions of dollars make a large sum. Invested at 5 per cent. interest it would produce nearly $2,000,000 per week. Then you see there are more than sixteen millions of horses and mules alone, and to feed and care for these it costs the modest sum of $4,000,000 per day. A little while ago a very clever and intelligent citizen of Indiana estimated that bad roads cost the farmer $15 per year for each horse and mule in his service. This means a loss in the aggregate of nearly $250,000,000 per year. Add wear and tear of wagons and harnesses, $100,000,000 ; depreciated value of farm lands $2,000,- 000,000 : total, *twenty-three hundred and fifty millions of dollars.*

Making the utmost allowance in favor of the farmer, and granting the necessity for the liberal use of horse-power in the maintenance of agricultural traffic, it is easily certain that the farmers of this country are keeping at least two millions of horses more than would be necessary to do all the hauling between farm and market, if only the principal roads were brought to a good condition. If you assume that each of these horses is fed the ordinary army ration of hay and oats, it requires 14,000 tons of hay or fodder, and seven hundred and fifty thousand bushels of oats per day to feed these unnecessary animals, which themselves have a money value of $140,000,000. The value of hay and oats fed to these horses per day is about $300,000,—or something like $114,000,000 per year.*

-- --

IV.

I was down at Hubmire's for a week last April, and we had an occasional friendly argument on this question of better roads. The wet weather had hung on, and the wagon roads were then in a desperate condition. Things were dull about the old farm and Hubmire had been dividing his time between chores and trout

* This computation is made by estimating the value of hay at $10 per ton, and oats at twenty-three cents per bushel ; these figures being close to the average values in the several States during the year 1889.

fishing to keep off the blues. One day he had to go to town.
There was something needed in the house and a dozen things to
be attended to which could not longer be put off. To kill as
many birds as possible with one stone, Hubmire hitched his team
to the box wagon with the intention of hauling out a load of coal
for the sitting-room stove. I hadn't seen a newspaper for more
than a week and was glad of this chance to connect with civilization and find out whether we hadn't skipped a day in the cal
endar ; so I accepted Hubmire's invitation and went with him.
It was a slow and painful trip. The clay roads were wet, bot-
tomless and sticky, and the horses struggled along in about the
same way that a fly wades in molasses. We passed only one
vehicle on all those six miles of road, and that was a hearse. It
was about half a mile out of town. The team was tied to the
fence, and, as we came up, we saw that the driver had left his
seat and gone back a short distance where he stood with a fence
picket in his hand, reaching out into the mud, and vainly trying
to recover an object which seemed to be sunk nearly out of sight
in the soft mire. It looked enough like a bottle to be one, but
the lone fisherman told Hubmire it was a plume-holder that had
"joggled loose," and dropped off the top of the hearse.

"That's Berriam, the undertaker," said Hubmire ; "Guess
he's goin' to plant somebody up in the Sokeville district."

"Yes," I replied, wiping a soft clay poultice out of my left
eye, "It will be easy digging up in the old graveyard ; I wonder
how Berriam found out the man was dead."

The subtlety of that joke was too deep for Hubmire. It had
never yet occurred to him that there was anything wrong with
the roads. He had never seen better ones, and he knew that these
were as good as the average, take it the state over.

It was the middle of the afternoon before we started for
home with our half load of coal, and when we reached the
"corners" Hubmire stopped at Rumsey's to water his horses and
give them a few minutes' rest. The season was a little in advance
of fly-time and Rumsey was taking a comfortable nap in his big
arm-chair in the barroom. Our conversation outside, together
with the noise of the pump-handle, roused Rumsey to the occasion, and, coming out to the doorway, he stretched his arms,
legs and jaws by a kind of simultaneous reaching out of all the
muscles, pulled his soft hat down in front till the rim made a

very sharp angle with the bridge of his nose, threw his head back
far enough to enable him to see straight ahead and said :

"Hello, Enoch ; glad to see you ; come in and warm up a
little ; how's the goin' down below ?"

"Nothin' to brag about," said Hubmire, looking at the sea of
paste which covered his horses and wagon ; "beats all what a
power of rain we've had this spring. How's business ?"

"Hain't made a dollar since the January thaw," said Rumsey;
"the mud is so terrible deep folks can't afford to be neighborly,

and when they do drop in they don't stop long. It takes about
all their time goin' and comin'."

We followed Rumsey into the front room of the hotel and
there was a solemn and musty air about the place which was very
impressive. It was a "public house" with a suspension of public
patronage. From four directions the roads ran in and centered
at Rumsey's. Good farming lands stretched away on all sides
and every natural condition was favorable to success ; but the
roads were indescribable. The farmers and country merchants
were surrounded and besieged by impassible sloughs of deep
mud, and business was wrecked by the bondage of bad roads.
Rumsey couldn't see it. He was born in it, reared in it, and it
had become a part of his existence. But Rumsey was genial.
He had an irrepressible load of good fellowship in his mental

cargo and was not disposed to quarrel with natural conditions—
of which, to his mind, the mud road was a familiar type. To him
all roads were dirt roads, for he had never seen any other. He
knew that water was wet, that dirt was soluble, that clay was
sticky, and he had always regarded slush and mortar as a kind of
visitation of Providence to mankind—"inscrutable" enough to
be sure; but nevertheless as certain and unavoidable as the
changing seasons themselves. So, in season and out, wet or dry,
busy or idle, Rumsey kept a placard over the pepper-sauce bottles
in his barroom which read:

> Welcome the coming, speed the parting guest."

V.

That night, when Hubmire had finished his work at the barn,
we sat together and smoked. I thought it was a good time to
talk with Hubmire about the roads; so I suggested to him that
he could do all his plowing and farm work with two horses, and
that if there was a good hard road running down to the village
he might do all his teaming without adding to that number;
that he was now feeding five horses when two or three ought to
be enough.

"Now don't," said Hubmire, "don't tell me I've got too
many horses; I think I know a thing or two about farmin', and I
tell you I hain't got horses enough. My bay team will haul a
smashin' good load of hay to town any day, and that's all any
man's team 'll do. I tell you I ain't askin' for better roads than
we've got right here in this township." Hubmire thinks a good
deal of himself and is a hard man to convince. He never takes a
drink at the town pump without first rinsing the dipper, inside
and out, and in matters of argument he is just as cautious not to
be contaminated by suspicious ideas. But I like Hubmire.
We've had many a good day's hunt together in old times, and
I've always found him a good companion and a humane sports-
man. He is an honest man and a good husband, and there's
always hope for a man like that.

So I kept up the fight. I said to him: "Hubmire, you are
wrong. I know you keep good horses; there are none better in
the county; everything about your farm is in the best condi-

tion, and there isn't a farmer in the country who has done more hard work in the last twenty years than you have done. Everything that you have found to be of value to the farmer you have added to your possessions, and if I could show you that a good road is the one thing necessary to improve your prosperity, you would be the loudest preacher for improved roads in this state. In spite of all your hard work you are not clear of debt. There is a mortgage on your farm and it draws interest night and day ; it eats into your prosperity ; there is something wrong with you and with all your neighbors. Farming is no longer as prosperous as it was in times gone by. The population of many of our agricultural districts is less than it was ten years ago ; the mortgage indebtedness of American farms is increasing at the rate of about eight and a half millions of dollars per year, and the decrease in farm value since 1880 is estimated at $200,000,000. In the single State of Ohio this loss amounted to about $7 per acre for the entire State, and there are other States where the proportion shows a still worse condition of affairs."

"The country is losing and the towns are gaining ; the farmers are growing poorer ; the government is growing richer. Every minute, night and day, the United States Government collects $178 more than it spends. Think of it. Ten thousand six hundred and eighty-six dollars per hour ; $256,320 per day ; $7,689,600 per month ; $93,556,800 per year. Something is wrong. It is not so in other countries. I have been looking it up, and I have at home, reports from more than twenty European countries relating to their internal affairs. In those countries the farmers prosper in about the same poportion that prosperity follows other lines of business ; agriculture holds its own, and there is no more independent class of people in those countries than the farmers."

"Now, singularly enough, the most striking difference between those countries and ours is found in the condition of the country roads. With them communication is easy and quickly accomplished. Their governments, instead of rolling up and hoarding a ridiculous surplus, spend large sums in the building and repairing of the country roads. The result is that in Europe the farmers drive 20 to 30 miles from home to market with immense loads, in all kinds of weather, at all seasons of the year, and return home the same day. The European horse hauls twice as much as an American horse, simply because the roads are much better. His owner can visit his neighbors at any time ; drive to town ; make social calls and enjoy all the personal advantages of a resident of the city, and still maintain the independence and enjoy the pleasures of country life."

"Nonsense." said Hubmire, "I'd like to see the fairyland you're talking about. I have got five as good horses as ever pulled a strap, and I know how to take care of them. I don't drive to town excepting when the roads are good, and ,then, for hauling loads, my horses won't take a back seat for any man."

"Hubmire," said I, with some impatience, "I see we can never agree on this question till we settle one important difference. You say you never drive to town until the roads are good. Now, leaving out the fact that you are losing plenty of good time while you wait for the mud to dry up, just tell me what you call a good road."

"Well," said Hubmire, "any road is good enough for my horses when the mud begins to stiffen up so it will pack and roll under the wheel."

"Then let me tell you, Hubmire," said I, "that you don't know what a good road is. You never saw a good road in all your life. A good road has no mud to dry, roll or pack. It is made hard and stays hard and smooth at all times of the year, and when once made it is easier and cheaper to keep in repair than any dirt road you ever saw." But Hubmire only smiled in his good-natured, doubting way, lighted his pipe and went out to see that everything about the place was snug and secure for the night.

VI.

That talk with Hubmire troubled me a good deal. He is counted a sensible man in the community where he lives, and I could see that his words reflected the judgment of thousands of farmers of whom he was an excellent type. The mud was then drying up in places, or, as Hubmire would say, it was beginning to "pack and roll under the wheel," and one day, a week later, Hubmire drove to town with his stout span of bays and a load of hay. It wasn't a very big load, for the roads were still rutty, and after Hubmire had got into the village the big bays were "packing and rolling" the ruts with a little too much vigor when one of the whiffletrees broke. Hubmire unhitched his team and drove down to the blacksmith's shop for necessary repairs, and while he was gone every horse and vagrant cow that came along nipped his load. It stood alone and unprotected, and here is a photograph of that load, showing it exactly as it was.

A month later I went up to see Hubmire again, feeling that I was somewhat better equipped to meet his peculiar style of

argument. I showed him this photograph of his abandoned load of hay.

"Hubmire," said I, "whenever I see an American farmer with a load of hay like that, I feel ashamed for my country. You hauled that load to market with your big bays. You thought the road was in fair condition, and it was one of those roads which you say is good enough because the 'mud will roll and pack under the wheel.' Right here is where we disagree. I told you awhile ago that the farm horses of Europe hauled twice as much as your horses, simply because the roads of that continent are better than ours. You seemed to ridicule the idea. I could not convince you by observation or experience and I have taken the trouble to bring you some pictures of European

roads, showing them exactly as they are to-day. I have been
fortunate enough to find one which admirably serves the case in
hand.   Here is a picture taken from a photograph of a French

road, showing a French farmer with his load of hay, on his way
to market, 9 miles distant."

   " It will do you good to look at this picture, and I am going
to leave it with you for a little while.   There are something like
4 tons of hay in that Frenchman's load, or about 1½ tons for
each horse. Notice the surface of the road. It is hard and
smooth, nicely sloped in both directions so as to insure quick
drainage ; the wheel tires are two and a half times as wide as
those on your wagon, and they roll over the surface of the road
in a manner that tends to make it hard and smooth instead of

cutting and creating ruts as is always the case when narrow tires are used. Notice the height of the load ; it towers up among the trees, and its immense bulk gives it the appearance of an American haystack ; compare its height with the height of the driver who walks along by the roadside or with the size of the chaise which you see coming along immediately behind. See how easily the horses jog along ; they are moving as comfortably as you can wish, and there is no sign of tugging or straining in their movements. If you had a road like that from your farm to town, you might do all your hauling with two horses instead of the five you now have and save yourself an immense expense."

" Now, I want to say to you, that the farmers of this country raised something like 45,000,000 tons of hay last year and every pound of that hay was moved at an expense of twice as much power as ought to be necessary ; and you must know, also, that this picture of a French road is by no means a special or uncommon one ; such roads may be found anywhere among the better countries of Europe. France alone has about 130,000 miles of roads practically as good as this one, and yet her territory is only about four times as large as that of the State of New York. That government spends $18,000,000 a year to keep these roads in repair. The French Republic has adopted an honest principle of state-craft by doing something from year to year in behalf of its farmers ; it proceeds upon the theory that these roads are the property and care of all the people ; that they are a public necessity and one of the institutions of the government ; that the farmers alone should not bear the burden of making and repairing these lines of travel, which reach from country to town, since the prosperity of both town and country depend upon their condition in a most emphatic degree ; that agriculture is everywhere the guage of national thrift and that the permanent enrichment of the Republic must depend upon the fullest development of its resources. There is a good deal worth thinking about in this matter of national policy. No country ever yet attained greatness whose farmers were not great, and in these days of improvement and driving competition, the farmer has the same right to demand means for saving time, space, power, materials and expense as are accorded by the government to other divisions of society."

VII.

I had many talks with Hubmire before I left the farm, and though he didn't seem to be quite convinced I could see that he had begun to think the matter over, and I am satisfied that Hubmire will work out a sound conclusion. He is a conservative fellow; but he has a slow, sure, tenacious and persevering way of thinking that is sure to land him on good ground when he starts in the right direction.

I have told you of my experience with Hubmire because he is, in many ways, a typical representative of your class, and what I said to him was, in my judgment, applicable to thousands of similar cases to be found in every county of the United States.

The American farmer has nerve, vigor, ambition, industry, good soil, good climate and every natural facility for the successful pursuit of agriculture; but the average American farm is a lonely institution. Its owner is separated from his neighbors, largely denied the many social advantages which belong to people who are able to mingle with each other from day to day, and kept at home from many gatherings, social, political and religious, from which he might receive both pleasure and benefit. His sons desert the farm for the more profitable and enlightened conditions of city life, and the allurement of profit which is held out in every community of successful farmers is not so conspicuous in the United States to-day as to entice our farmer's sons from the greater promise of success offered by mercantile occupations.

Farm property is no longer in active demand, and investments which in other years would have sought the security afforded by farm mortgages are now directed in other channels. Go to any of the large cities of the Union and you will find upon the books of the real estate dealers an endless array of notices of farms for sale or to exchange for city property.

But I did not intend to digress. It will interest you to know more about the roads of France. In that country there is no such diversity between the material progress of the farmer and that of the merchant—between the country and the town—as is found in this country. The farmers prosper and have always prospered. Every dollar spent by the French Govern-

ment to bring itself more closely in touch with its rural population, has been well invested. You remember that terrible war
when from Prussia the King, the warrior and the statesman led
the German legions across the breadth of the French Empire
and forced the capitulation of Paris; and how the brave French-
men were humiliated by the exacting terms of peace which their
conquerors imposed. The immense tribute demanded by the
Germans at the close of that war, now twenty years ago, was
made up from moneys contributed in a wonderful degree by the
French farmers, and the admiration of the world which their
patriotism excited in the payment of that tribute, was not greater
than the wonder which everybody felt at the ready thrift which
had enabled them to meet such enormous demands.

Here is a picture showing a valley near one of the small
villages in the interior of France. The scene is about 50 miles
northwesterly from Paris, not far from Amiens, which many
years ago was a fortified city; but the ramparts have been tore
down and replaced by splendid roadways, adding to the beauty

and thrift of the city and to the convenience and pleasure of its people.

In the foreground you see the same kind of hard, smooth road that is shown in the last picture. In the distance, running down from the hills and through the valley, you see a white line of road, showing the various directions in which these roads run and the uniform appearance which their hard finished surfaces present.

Of course these roads of France are not built by farmers who " work out " their highway taxes after the manner followed in

this country, nor are they repaired by the use of plows, hoes or scrapers like those which are brought into use at the annual farmer's picnic which takes place when you go out to " work the road " in your township. On the contrary, they are built and kept up under a system which is perhaps the most perfect in the world. There is an official-in-chief, who takes charge of all the main roads of the Republic and requires from his subordinates complete reports at frequent intervals. In this manner information is always at hand showing the condition of the roads in all parts of the country. Of course, the work is divided into different sections, which, in turn, are in charge of subordinate engineers or superintendents. Broken stone is furnished by contract, and considering the amount of labor accomplished each year on the French roads, the cost is surprisingly small. The roads of our own states, at least the important roads, should be maintained in the same way. The inefficient, haphazard and ridiculously expensive method which we have followed for the last hundred years, should have convinced us by this time of the necessity of change. Of course I may be wrong about this, because it has never yet been determined just how long it takes a great and intelligent people to twist itself out of the rut of an accepted and established blunder. Upon this point, a keen and witty observer of public affairs says : "A hundred years is a very little time for the duration of a national error, and it is so far from being reasonable to look for its decay at so short a date, that it can hardly be expected, within such limits, to have displayed the full bloom of its imbecility."

VIII.

When I write to you about these roads of Europe I know that you are apt to believe that these European countries are more wealthy than ours ; that they are more thickly populated ; more thoroughly cultivated ; and that these splendid roads are built for the accommodation of only those farmers whose lands are highly cultivated ; but in this you are wrong. France is divided into eighty-seven "departments" or political divisions, which, in many respects, are not unlike our counties. In eighty-one of these eighty-seven departments the population per square mile is less than that of the State of Rhode Island ; in seventy-eight it is less than the population per square mile of Massachusetts ; in sixty-six it is less than that of New Jersey, while if you take the combined area of New York, Pennsylvania, Connecticut, Massachusetts, Rhode Island and New Jersey it will appear that the average population per square mile of these States exceeds that of seventy out of the eighty-seven departments of France. Many of these departments in France are less populous than the thickly settled counties in our western States, but the uniform excellence of the roads is everywhere maintained. On page 24 is a picture taken in one of the forests of France, where you see

no signs of cultivation and where many of the best farms are in
fact some miles distant from town.

You see in this picture the same excellent quality of road as
that which appears in the ones I have already shown you.

Many years ago the French farmer had the same method of
making and repairing the wagon roads that is followed in your

county to-day. He quit farming for several days each year and
" worked out " his road tax.

Do you think he could be induced to go back to the old
style of doing things ? Look at the picture on this page, copied
from a photograph of a French road taken last year on the day
after a heavy rain storm. The road surface is smooth and dry ;
the tall poplars on either side have been trimmed to the upper
branches so as to let in the sun and air and hasten the drying of

the road after a storm. Then notice the heaps of broken stone on each side of the road. These are used by the workmen in making constant repairs from day to day whenever the least imperfection appears.

In Belgium also the principal roads are built and maintained by the general government, and in 1880 in the nine provinces of Belgium over 79 per cent. of the highroads were of this class, the entire length of high-class roads being 3,173 English miles, out of a total of five thousand two hundred and eighty-six miles of roads of all classes. The best roads of Belgium are in the provinces of Namur, Liège and Luxembourg, and permanent employees are kept on the roads under the directions of the chief engineer of the province, for the purpose of insuring the observance of the regulations and looking after the constant repair of the highways.

In Baden the main roads are under the supervision of the State authorities, and are cared for with a studious regard for the requirements of the farmer and inland travel. Under the law relating to roads in Baden, the duty of maintaining the road falls as follows: One quarter each upon the parish (town) and district (county) in which the road is situated. The remaining one-half upon the State treasury.

In Hesse-Darmstadt the roads are divided into two classes, called state roads and district roads, of which the former are a direct care and charge upon the general government, and when the district roads become so important as to require the attention of state officers, they can, under direction of the district assembly ("Kreistag") be declared state roads. Every district is bound to appoint the necessary officials connected with the district roads. These officials consist of a skilled person who must be capable of filling the office of district overseer and a proper force of laborers requisite for the work in hand. Annual sums are allotted to each province out of the state budget to pay the cost of making and maintaining the public roads.

In Italy the Minister of Public Works is at the head of the Department of Public Roads. The construction of these roads is, in most cases, undertaken by contracts, the work being carried on under direction of government engineers. These contracts extend also to the work of maintenance and repair, and include the transport of materials, the cost of earth works, embankments, drainage, masonry, ironwork, stonework, removal of

snow, mud and dust and the care of border trees planted along
the sides of the highways.   The contractor is bound to deposit a
fixed sum of money in the hands of the public officials, to insure
the performance of his contract, and, on the termination of a
contract, the road must be delivered up in perfect order and
repair to answer the description contained in the specifications,
and all defects becoming apparent within one month thereafter

COUNTRY ROAD IN ITALY.

are made good at the cost of the contractor, under an estimate
of the chief engineer of the district.   The money deposit of the
contractor is only returned to him upon the compliance of all
the terms of his contract and in case of his neglect or refusal to
execute the orders conveyed to him by the highway officials, the
latter have power to direct the necessary work to be carried on
at the expense of the contractor.   A repetition of such offense or
the perpetration of any fault on the part of the contractor, results
in the termination of his contract and the confiscation of his
money deposit.   The Government road laborers are called " cantonniers " and are selected with great care, special reference
being had to character and honesty.   They must be of robust

constitution and must be able to read and write. Each one of these cantonniers is provided with a full set of tools and implements specified by law. His hours of work are from sunrise to sunset, and each day he is obliged to go over the entire track of road placed in his charge. He must be constantly upon the line of his work in all kinds of weather, and, in case of necessity, is bound to work on public holidays. His chief duties are the levelling and repair of the highways ; the removal of snow, mud, dust, etc. He must assist travelers in distress and vehicles disabled by accident or by weather, and for any neglect of duty he may be fined, suspended or dismissed, according to the degree of the offense. The fines accumulated during the year are divided among the deserving cantonniers or given to one of the mutual benefit associations, of which they are members. Cantonniers who serve with credit and distinction for three or more years are promoted and given an increase of monthly wages. In the five years 1873 to 1878, Italy spent about $16,000,000 on her roads, although before that appropriation was made, many excellent highways existed in all parts of the kingdom. In 1881 Italy constructed about 120 miles of new roads and had then about 11,040 miles in course of construction. Mentioning the policy of the Italian Government with respect to its maintenance of the public roads, Mr Beauclerk, representing the British Government at Rome in the year 1882, in his official report to the home cabinet, said : "It is therefore evident that the Italian Government are doing their utmost to develop rapidly and extensively the means of ccmmunication in the kingdom, and there is little doubt that the large outlay incurred, is fully justified by the increased prosperity and wealth of the country." At that time, something more than 5,000 miles of roads were in charge of the Italian Government. More than twenty-five hundred cantonniers were employed and their services were devoted to the care of all the national roads, except five.

In the Netherlands, as in the countries already mentioned, the principal roads are maintained at the expense of the State.

In Portugal a similar rule is adopted. The State takes the responsibility of the construction, maintenance and service of all important roads connecting the provincial capital and the principal frontier towns. The director of public works and skilled engineers have the principal direction of the Government work, relating to the common roads.

(TO BE CONTINUED.)

NATIONAL HIGHWAYS.

BY ALBERT MOTT, C. E.

NE of our country's great ministers of finance,—one who was a statesman and political economist,—left as a deathbed legacy, these words : " The history of all civilized countries attests the fact that the nation best equipped in these respects (means of communication), rapidly becomes the most powerful, the richest and the most prosperous." This opinion was the result of many years of study and service to the United States Government, by the Honorable Wm. Windom, who closed his earthly career as Secretary of the Treasury. Said that profound constitutional lawyer, Daniel Webster, in the Senate of the United States : "I look upon a road over the Alleghanies, a canal around the falls of the Ohio, or a canal or railway from the Atlantic to the western waters, as being an object large and extensive enough to be fairly said to be for the common benefit."

It is generally, nay, it is universally conceded, that good roads are an absolute necessity in the economy of a nation : that they are actually investments which give a return justifying the initial expense and maintenance. In some localities and for short distances they successfully compete with railroads, water courses and other means of transportation. In magnificent distances they act as feeders to the other transportation routes. They are the greatest factors in the problem of economy to the agriculturist, and to every business enterprise that results in a product to be hauled. They are absolute essentials to the military features of a vast nation where large masses of men, artillery and munitions of war are to be moved, and at the same time, act for its own protection during transit in the presence of an enemy.

The United States treasury profits by the prosperity of the people of the country. Funds appropriated for internal improvement, is an investment paying such enormous margins as would excite the envy of the money kings. It does already induce the opposition of railroads on parallel lines of water courses, although they encourage the investments in harbors at their

terminals. In one of the harbors of the country, the United
States Government invested several hundred thousand dollars
in deepening and widening the channel marked out by nature, and
thereby increased its custom receipts from about two millions
to nearly eight millions of dollars in gold. Internal improvements facilitating and cheapening hauling and transportation of
bulky products, are profitable to the general government.

In improving the waterways of the country, it is the custom
of the government to make one great channel or thoroughfare
to which connections can be made by private enterprise. In the
same manner, highways on land to principal points would be
excellent investments in creating national thoroughfares, and
would be the means of inviting and even inducing state, county
and private enterprise to intersect and make available for themselves the great channel of commerce. The government has
constructed, and to-day, under appropriations granted by Congress, is constructing national roads—not "post roads," but
national highways within the confines of States. That these
roads are insignificant as to grandeur in mileage distances, does
not alter the fact that the constitutional principle involved is
conceded by the legislation. The principle is also emphasized by
the fact that due consideration, debate and reference to authorities including that autocrat of constitutional interpretation, the
Supreme Court of the United States, was given by the legisla-
tors when dealing with the question.

Wagon roads are the feeders of the markets, the railroads,
the marine channels of communication and commerce of the
world. Every person, every profession and every line of business is directly or indirectly interested, and the revenues of the
United States Government the most. The government is a
business concern, and must profit by its investment the same as
any other. It is not to be expected that it will profit if it does
not invest. While people may differ in opinion as to the most
proper means of procuring the same end, all agree that the
end should be attained in some way of providing the country
with good roads. If an additional and more rapid means of
obtaining the result lies in the direction of national action, then
it would seem to be folly to ignore it.

In the crusade for highway improvement in this country,
which had its initial at the hands of The League of American

Wheelmen, the policy has necessarily been the slow one of agitation and education of the masses to the standard that would give a due comprehension of the intrinsic value of good roads in the everyday business and pleasure of the individual, the general prosperity accomplished by them in which all participate ; the demand for legislation which such an education creates, and the pushing of road enactments in the legislative halls of the different States. In brief, education creates the demand, and the demand naturally contemplates legislation. In a work of education, the kindergarten system of object lessons is not to be lightly ignored. Such object lessons would be the construction of national highways to principal points, and they would more quickly educate the people than any other process in the whole curriculum. As the general government would profit enormously by the education of its citizens in this respect, it follows naturally that the funds expended would be an excellent business investment and justifiable in every conceivable way. The general government also has the civic machinery at hand to build national roads without the additional expense of employing engineering talent. Having educated its own engineers, and paying them regular salaries which are not increased or diminished by the modesty or magnitude of the duties they are called upon to perform, the additional duty of building roads would be undertaken by the United States with a well equipped corps of engineers, who already have charge of the other works of internal improvement, and who are specially trained in similar enterprises undertaken by the government.

As this article was opened by a quotation from one statesman, it may well be closed by the golden words of another. President Madison, in a message to Congress, wrote : " Among the means of advancing the public interests, the occasion is a proper one for recalling the attention of Congress to the general importance of establishing throughout our country the roads and canals *which can best be executed under the national authority*. No objects within the circle of political economy so richly repay the expenses bestowed on them ; there are none, the utility of which is more universally ascertained and acknowledged ; none that do more honor to the Government whose wise and enlarged patriotism duly appreciates them. Nor is there any country which presents a field where nature invites more the art of man to complete her own work for their accommodation and benefit. These considerations are strengthened, moreover, by the political effect of these facilities for inter-communication, in bringing and binding more closely together the various parts of our extended confederacy. While the States individually, with a laudable enterprise and emulation, avail themselves of their local advantages by new roads, by navigable canals, and by improving the streams susceptible of navigation, the general Government is the more urged to similar undertakings, requiring a national jurisdiction and national means, by the prospect of thus systematically completing so inestimable a work."

THE PERSONAL LABOR SYSTEM OF ROAD TAX.

BY CASPER TABOTT.

A TAX is the tribute which savagery pays to civilization; the entrance fee to community life; the price we pay for the privilege of living together, and for the right to fly a national flag. Your typical hermit is forever a typical sloven. He harbors no ambition, holds no visible property, needs no defence, seeks no friends, grooms himself but once a year—and pays no taxes. Like every other citizen who uses the public property without contributing to the public coffers, he is more or less a sponge. He is simply a little lower in the social scale because he enjoys the common benefits provided by the common laws, and permits his neighbors to foot the bill. He is beyond the dignifying influence of the public tax.

Now the methods and influences of every organized society entail upon its members certain burdens, and these are usually in some measure commensurate with the advantages enjoyed. For all the privileges of citizenship we tax ourselves in two ways: First, in our ambition to appear well, and to display evidences of our acquirements and abilities, we tax ourselves to pay for a thousand of the conveniences and luxuries of social life, and we pay compliment to our friends and at the same time satisfy our own vanity by expending money in the clothing and adorning of our persons and in the embellishment of our homes. Secondly, we pay another kind of tax, infinitely smaller in amount, yet always more grudgingly expended—a tax which goes to pay for those things which we cannot personally own, nor personally pay for, and which become our property only in a kind of reflective way. This is the public tax—the money paid under an assessment designed to be equitable, and intended, not for the enrichment of the individual, but for the maintenance of the commonwealth, and the improvement of those several institutions which are created for the common good. The selfish instincts in the human mind leads us to despise this tax, and its collection is each year carried on by a sort of cork-screw process, which is alike disagreeable to the official who collects and to the citizen who pays.

Once in a life-time some social reformer whose benevolent instinct is abnormally developed, tries to lead the way to a kind of communistic reform by which each person may be induced to contribute all his gains to the public granary, and take his living with all the rest of mankind, of high and low degree, out of the public trough. But the venal impulse prevails, and to the Utopian scheme of the communist, the average citizen gives answer after the manner of the old corn law rhyme :

> "What is a communist? One who hath yearnings
> For equal division of unequal earnings;
> Idler, or bungler, or both ; he is willing
> To fork out his penny and pocket your shilling."

And so the prominence of self is the prevailing thing to be recognized in the treatment of public questions, and every reform which promises benefit must promise that benefit to the individual.

But every individual taxpayer has an interest in the way in which the public taxes are expended and the public institutions maintained. He is a shareholder of the body politic—a part owner of the corporate property which the State controls. In this view of the case let us consider the road tax question. The common road is not, in fee, owned by the public. It is commonly a strip of land, a line of travel, in which the public has acquired an easement, a right to travel perpetually for all the purposes of inter-communication and traffic, and wherever a

state has been erected by the adoption of an organic law, some
provision has usually followed for the construction and maintenance of these lines of public travel. When the United States
became a nation it was easy and simple to adopt colonial
methods, and as these methods related in some respects to the
use and keeping of the common roads, it was an easy step to
borrow the road laws of England, since England was the
mother of the colonies. At that time there were few better
roads than the English roads—and none worse. There were
better road laws than those of England ; but, not being printed
in the English language, they had little claim upon the American affection, if indeed they had any place within the field of
American knowledge. So we adopted the English law and the
English dirt road. That law, like a hundred others on the English statute books, has outlived its usefulness. It was a relic of
feudalism, involving a system of statute labor which was born
of an ignorant brain and suited only to answer conditions of
national poverty or a system of serfdom. In the early days of
the republic the fortunes of war and the undeveloped condition
of the country compelled us to subscribe to the first of these
conditions, and to yield to the embarrassments which it imposed. We were poor, individually and collectively, and might
well have been excused for attempting to "work" our own
highways, even in that crude and unsystematic way which the
passing century has bred within us as a national habit. But we
have long since outlived the pains and trials of national infancy.
The American greenback holds a front rank in the financial pro-
cession, and our national treasury is being enriched at the rate
of a hundred millions or so a year. Every species of public
debt, national, state, county, and town, has largely decreased
within the last decade ; the savings banks of the country report
a large increase in the number of individual depositors, as well
as a corresponding swelling of the funds deposited, and every
kind of industry seems to have been enriched in value and quick-
ened in its operations by the development of population, and by
the adoption of the thousand and one methods and appliances
which forever seek a market in populous centres. Save only the
farmer. He and his industry are beyond the stimulating influences of most modern inventions, and while it is true that his
methods of tillage and harvesting have been improved and

lightened by the use of machinery, it is no less certain that the general prosperity of the farmer has not kept pace with that of other branches of society, and that the allurement of gain is no longer conspicuously prominent in the general field of American agriculture. Indeed it is quite safe to say that the American farm, in general, is not increasing in value.

It is well worth while to inquire why this is so. The value of farm produce is not essentially less than in former years. The methods of farm work have been lightened by improved appliances, and from the farmer's standpoint, the conditions are quite as favorable as at any time in the history of the country. But from the standpoint of the business man and the investor, other lines of business offer more substantial promise. The value of farm property in these days must depend not only upon the quality of the land, its productive qualities and its location, but it must be considered also with a special view of the lines of communication which connect it with the market. Delays, uncertainties, the amount of power required, unnecessary expense and useless wear and tear are important questions with the capitalist and the investor of these days, and every obstacle which stands in the way of constant and regular business transactions, is a blemish which no shrewd tradesman will tolerate.

This obstacle, to the American farmer, is the common dirt road. By long use, and through ignorance of a better kind, he has learned to endure this sort of highway, and he has not yet learned that in all the route from the home farm to the ultimate consumer, the dirt road which leads from his dooryard to the railway station is the line of greatest resistance, and that which imposes upon him and his neighbors not only the chief burden of transportation, but which is maintained at a cost far exceeding that which is required to keep in repair the best roads of modern Europe. It all comes from our adherence to the antiquated and ridiculous idea of "working out" the road tax. Every road is a structure and needs a foundation. A good road was never built by accident, nor maintained by ignorance. It is quite as senseless and futile to attempt to build and maintain a good highway by the calling out of A, B, and C from their various personal occupations to maul and scrape a few miles of soft dirt with hoes and shovels, as it would be to expect the same persons, under a similar system, to contribute their

personal labor in the successful erection of a state house or a
county penitentiary. In either case the proper completion of
the work would require that it be done under an intelligent
head and by persons whose knowledge or instruction fitted them
for that kind of employment. Moreover it may be said that
besides these objections, the system of "working out" road
taxes presents certain features which are inequitable as among
the citizens themselves. The money collected from those persons
who elect to pay their assessment in money rather than by
personal labor is, in many cases, diverted to mysterious uses
which only the town politicians have power to disclose ; while,
on the other hand, the labor performed here and there by that
little squad of farmers who count their time so cheaply as to
render it in the public service for the sake of saving a dollar a
day, is generally applied where it is likely to tend to their
personal benefit, without regard to the general requirements of
public travel. I believe I run no risk of successful contradiction
in saying that the money and labor spent by the people in the
State of New York alone within the last half century in the
keeping of one of the vilest systems of dirt roads on the face of
the earth would more than suffice to build and maintain fifty
thousand miles of the best macadam roads that modern skill
could produce. The simple fact is that under the present
system the money is squandered and the labor misapplied,
wasted and practically thrown away. Drainage, grading and
every elementary idea involved in the making and keeping of a
good road is ignored, and the work is done without rule, reason,
or any regard for ultimate results. On every mile of dirt road
sixteen feet wide within the settled portions of the United
States there falls each year nearly nine thousand tons of water.
What becomes of it ? Under the present enlightened system of
"working out " road taxes, we permit this water to stand for
months at a time in great pools, and proceed to churn and mix
it with the soft dirt by the use of narrow wheel tires till the
fierce days of summer carry off this water by the slow process
of evaporation, and then, in the easy and opportune time, we
apply the lazy process of squaring our road tax account with
the public by a kind of shiftless tinkering, which makes the
road even worse in summer and leaves it all the more susceptible to the dissolving influences of the autumn showers. The

system is all wrong.   Other nations have long since abandoned it.   Their farming properties have improved in value, and the payment of road taxes in money under a system which requires that the highways shall be properly made and properly kept throughout the year has produced such amazing results in the enhancement of rural conditions that no kind of argument could induce the European farmer to accept the drawbacks and embarrassments of the old system.

To sum up the whole matter the personal labor system of maintaining, the public roads is a travesty and a failure.   It has been tried everywhere and has never succeeded anywhere.   It may be safely asserted that since the foundation of the American Government there has never been a single mile of strictly first class road built and maintained under this system.   It is a blot upon our civilization, a scourge upon the industry of the farmer and upon every town surrounded by a farming popula-tion.   It is the most expensive to maintain, the least efficient in its uses, and it produces a road the most exasperating in its normal condition of all the roads ever contrived by the human hand.   It is degrading to the state and to the citizen whose personal labor it demands in the public service, for it is well to remember that the only two classes of persons of whom labor is exacted under statute law in payment of an obligation to the state, are the farmers who work upon the public highway and the criminals who perform labor in the common prisons.   The American farmer deserves at the hands   of his state a more elevating, a more equitable and a more efficient law.   Let us away with the old system, and, following the later and time proved methods of other countries, place at least our main roads under the charge and direction of skilled officials, and im-pose upon the State at large the obligation of keeping them in suitable repair.

RAILROADS AND WAGON ROADS.

N the planning and construction of a new railroad, that location is generally sought which is deemed most likely to contribute to its carrying trade and to this end its alignment is carried as far as possible through populous centres and through those regions where the natural conditions are such as to invite an increased population and the development of agriculture and traffic. In many cases, where the surrounding country is of a substantially uniform character, it is not uncommon to reckon that the carrying trade of the railroad will receive its contributions from a strip of territory of say three, five or ten miles in width, as the case may be, and located upon either side of the railroad line. Beyond the limit of this width it has been generally assumed that the difficulties of land travel, the cost of hauling produce over the ordinary wagon roads of the country and the usual handicaps imposed upon this kind of traffic by the uncertain conditions of the weather, during long seasons of the year, will bar the farmer and the tradesman from establishing a regular connection with the railroad market, and compel them to establish a more limited market in the smaller inland towns. The experienced railroad projector seldom goes astray in his calculations, and in these particulars the history of the American railroad has verified his view. If you travel along the route of any of the great trunk lines belonging to the American railroad system, you will find that the local freight business, immense as it may appear in the aggregate, is a very reliable barometer in the determination of the rural weather and a most exact indication of the condition of the country roads. If you will stop off for a day in the market town of any farming district, through which one of these railroads may happen to pass, you may learn from the local freight agent, not only that the farm produce delivered by the farmers at his station is hauled from a territory limited by the radius of a few miles, but that for weeks at a time in the rainy seasons of the year the delivery of this produce is practically

stopped, and that during such seasons nothing but the very re-
finement of financial extremity can induce a farmer to attempt
the journey from his home to the railway station.   Three
things result : first, the territory which contributes to the carrying trade of the railroad at each one of these hundreds of
country towns is extremely limited, owing to the miserable
quality and uncertain condition of the country roads ; secondly,
even this limited territory becomes a dead and passive factor in
its relations to the railroad traffic whenever the rains of fall and
spring make these roads impassable ; and thirdly, the depressed
condition of trade which, in every country town, is brought
about by the succession of farm traffic during these seasons,
reacts, in some measure, upon the railroad and upon the condition of its local business.   The object lesson which these facts
instill into the mind of the local freight agent might well be im-
pressed upon the attention of the railroad manager.   In the same
way that rivulets and brooks carry their contents to the swelling
tide of the great river, so the common wagon roads of the country
are the lines of traffic which contribute their loads to swell
the freighting business of the great railroads.

That these highways should be improved and developed; that
they should be constructed and repaired under a thoroughly
competent system and by competent persons is of greater importance to the railroad proprietors than they seem to commonly
understand.

Let us look at it from a technical standpoint : if we
assume that a radius of three miles is made to describe a
circle having the railway station as a centre, and that the territory within this circle is all that may be depended upon to
contribute its products regularly and with certainty to the
freighting business of the railroad, we may easily compute that
this area will include about 18,000 acres, or say 180 farms of the
average size of 100 acres each.   Of course the common roads
which extend in different directions throughout this three mile
circle are always carried beyond its limits into the surrounding
territory where, by various cross roads, connection is made with
the main routes leading to the market town.   What would be
the effect of improving these highways so that the radius of the
contributing circle should be increased to six miles instead of
three ?   The new circle, by that rule of mathematics which de-

fines the superficial ratio of one circle to another, would contain
four times the area of the inner circle, or to be more explicit,
it would contain over 72,000 acres or about 724 farms of 100
acres each, of which only one-quarter would be included within
the inner three mile circle, and the remaining three-quarters
(over 54,000) would belong to the surrounding belt. In productive capacity the extended territory would equal about
5,500,000 bushels of potatoes, or in corn, 1,140,000 bushels,
or in hay a little over 65,000 tons.

Of course, with the further enlargement of the contributing
belt, an immense increase of contributing products will again
result. It is hardly worth while to pursue the mathematical feature of this question, for it will be evident to every reader that
even a moderate improvement of the radial highways leading to
the country railroad station will tend largely to increase the
volume and insure the regularity of its country traffic, both as
to freight and passengers.

In still another respect—an unmistakable one—is the development of good roads of importance to the railroads with which
they connect. I refer now to the increase of trade, population,
and wealth among the town communities which are fortunate
enough to secure an improvement of the suburban roads by
which they are immediately surrounded. The measure of this
benefit to the railroads cannot be determined by mathematical
formula ; but by the proof of experience it has been so abun-
dantly established that no prudent man in these days will attempt to gainsay it. In New Jersey, Rhode Island, Massachusetts, Indiana, and other states where road improvement has
been carried on in the vicinity of railroad towns, these beneficent
results to the town and to the railroads have followed without
exception. The demand for suburban property seems to be the
certain result which follows the improvement of suburban lines
of communication, and in each case the facilities offered by good
roads for the constant and regular passage of country traffic,
has enhanced the prosperity of the market town, enlarged the pro-
portions of its market trade, invited the production of larger crops
to answer to the increased demands, and added to the social as
well as to the material condition of all the people within the
widened influence of these improved roads. To the thoughtful
railroad man these considerations will have abundant force. In

many of our states, the rapid development of railroad construction has carried us to a point where the building of new lines cannot now be profitably undertaken, and it would seem as though no better policy could be undertaken in the development of railroad traffic than that which looks to increasing the trade of existing lines. The building of American railroads at the outset was made possible, and the investment of railroad capital, encouraged by the liberal enactments of both national and state governments, and while it would be idle to expect these railroads to contribute to the improvement of state roads as a matter of mere sentiment, it is quite easy to see that from their standpoint as investors, it would well pay the great railroad companies of the United States to lend their aid and influence to the education of the people at large upon the question of better roads, and to the securing of that class of legislation by which the uniform and systematic improvement of the common roads may be brought about.

WARDEN (of insane asylum):—This poor woman imagines she is shopping all the time. Sometimes she sits in silence for whole weeks.

VISITOR:—What is she doing then?

WARDEN:—It is supposed that she imagines she is waiting for change.—*Cloak Review.*

YE STICKER AND YE STUCK.

GOD made two classes of mankind,
  Ye sticker and ye stuck;
Ye first is made of finest clay,
  YE last is made of muck.
Ye sticker hath ye royal time,
  And hath ye untold hoard;
But ye poorer little one he stuck
  Hath no more "tick" for board.
Right jolly is ye sticker man,
  He beeth broad and stout;

He liveth on ye fattest things,
  And driveth round about.
But ye poorer stuck doth never laugh,
  He groweth lean and lank;
And seeth all his pennies fade,
  In yonder failing bank.
God made ye classes as they are,
  I doubt not He knows best;
But still ye sticker man gets all
  And pulleth down ye vest.

          —*Philadelphia Press.*

A WORD of introduction. The creed, politics, purpose and declaration of principles of this publication may all be declared by the two words of its title, GOOD ROADS. It is the sole property of the national body of the League of American Wheelmen, and no other person, copartnership, or corporation, has any pecuniary claim, lien or ownership, either present or prospective, in any of its property, funds or material affairs. It will be issued from the Bureau of Roads Improvement, founded by the Executive Committee of the League and devoted to pushing the roads improvement reform with more extended facilities and upon a broader basis than has ever before been attempted within the United States.

Although published and maintained by the efforts of the League at large, GOOD ROADS will invite the co-operation of all good citizens who favor the move for improved highways, and especially will it ask and expect the support of those citizens whose business and property will receive pecuniary benefit by the improvement of the public roads and streets. To the wheelmen of the League and to the wheelmen of America we make special appeal for that hand-in-hand support which our fraternal relations give us a right to expect, and upon which the success of this magazine must in a great measure depend. In the discussion of League affairs and the affairs of wheelmen we shall aim to exclude from our columns all matter of a partisan or offensive nature, and shall confine such discussion to that branch of League work which pertains to the improvement of the public highways.

We shall publish from time to time articles from men of commanding ability and position, and such articles will be selected and given place solely with the view of their value to our reading columns and their interest to the general reader.

In the pursuit of this policy, if we are sometimes forced to exclude contributions from members of the League, it must be remembered that we look solely to the establishment of a successful and influential magazine, and that in the attainment of that object we must hold to a higher motive than the gratifying of that pleasure which comes from showing favor to our friends and brothers. GOOD ROADS will be illustrated, and with the progress of time we expect to make the pictorial feature of the magazine of special force and value. Everybody will concede the wisdom of this, for all the world loves a picture, and when a picture can be made to both entertain and instruct its measure of usefulness is doubled. Buckle says: " For one person who can think, there are at least a hundred persons who can observe. An accurate observer is no doubt rare; but an accurate thinker is far rarer. * * And, inasmuch as thinkers are more prone to accumulate ideas, while observers are more prone to accumulate facts, the overwhelming predominance of the observing class is a decisive reason why induction, which begins with facts, is always more popular than deduction, which begins with ideas."

And so, concurring in the idea expressed in the somewhat pedantic phrases of Mr. Buckle, we shall court the attention of the observer, by pictorial illustrations, of those facts which go to prove the necessity of better roads, and which the American field will tend to supply in such enticing quantities. And now, with confidence, we ask the indulgence of our friends and readers for those errors and shortcomings into which our uncertain efforts in a new venture will be likely to lead us.

We have sometimes wondered why it is that in the line of public improvement, and especially those improvements which affect the agricultural population, the United States Government has been so slow to avail itself of the advanced ideas and methods which seem to be adopted and taken up so quickly by foreign countries when once the value of these improvements has been established. We have received some enlightenment on this question by examining the report of Secretary Rusk, of the Department of Agriculture, for the year 1890. From this report it appears that the Department of Agriculture is practically without any representation abroad, and that the march of improvements, which in other departments have kept pace with the genius of France and England, has been crippled and neglected in that branch of the public service which is specially designed to serve the interests of the farmer. Secretary Rusk says:

"I desire to record here very emphatically my conviction that some method must be adopted by which, as occasion requires and without long delays, this Department shall be enabled to send representatives to foreign countries, in cases where only personal visits can be relied on to secure much needed information. The subject of world-wide competition has been dwelt upon at length on so many occasions that it would be purely superfluous to insist here upon the active competition which meets our own farmers in every market where their products are offered for sale.

* * * * * *

It may be well, perhaps, in this connection, to call attention to the fact that we are in this respect far behind the other nations of the world, however disagreeable it may be to confess it. Important gatherings of men devoted to agricultural science, and enjoying, by the courtesy of the government under whose jurisdiction they assemble, every privilege and facility for gaining information in regard to the agriculture of that country, are constantly being held in various parts of the world, at which representatives of this, the greatest agricultural country in the world, are conspicuous by their absence. * * A most notable instance of our omissions in this respect was furnished during the meeting last September of an international agricultural congress at Vienna, in which we had been especially invited to participate by the Austro-Hungarian Gov-

ernment, at which over eleven hundred delegates were present, including distinguished representatives of agricultural interests from every country in Europe, from Japan, from Australia, from India, and from South America, and at which were discussed subjects of profound interest to American agriculture. This was a meeting at which, for many reasons, it was most desirable that the United States, through this Department, should have been officially represented. Unfortunately, for want of adequate provision, the United States alone, of all the leading countries of the world, was absent. Let me here recall the fact, that since I had the honor to assume the office of Secretary of Agriculture, I have been visited by gentlemen from Austro-Hungary, Germany, Bavaria, France, Great Britain, Canada, Australia, New Zealand, Japan, and even from one of the native principalities of the East Indies, the official representatives of departments analagous to my own in their native countries, traveling under orders from, and under pay of their respective governments, armed with all the official credentials necessary to secure to them every attention and courtesy necessary to the prosecution of their inquiries. Thus do these countries indicate their willingness to learn whatever we may be able to teach them. Thus do they recognize the fact upon which I have already insisted—that there is an intellectual, as well as a commercial competition, to which the old maxim, 'knowledge is power,' applies with a force which all must recognize."

Yes, it is much that way. Our ministers and consuls represent the government in the important cities and towns of other countries, and their connection with the home department of state is intimate and important. Our treasury is guarded and our securities handled with a skill which any government on earth might emulate. Our munitions of war and military methods are kept to the highest standard, and we are building a navy which promises well to rival the powerful navies of Europe ; but we are forgetting that a few thousand dollars out of our fat treasury might well be spent in the study and adoption of those means and methods which quicken the internal industry of the country and enhance the condition and prospects of our rural population. And, incidentally, a few lessons in road making might not be astray in the pursuit of this sort of knowledge.

LAWS AND LEGISLATION

FROM the thirteenth senatorial district of New York (comprising the counties of Orange and Sullivan), comes gratifying news of the re-election of Senator William P. Richardson to the state senate. His sturdy warfare during the last two years in the cause of roads improvement, and the marked change of sentiment on this subject within the legislative halls at Albany, have made him the target for numerous mossback criticisms, and for the first time in the history of the state, the roads improvement question became an active factor in the election of a member of the legislature. Senator Richardson has not only been re-elected by more than double his former majority, but is the only republican senator in the state who goes back to Albany with an increased majority. We have before us a letter written by Senator Richardson, under date November 28th, in which he says:

"I made the fight in my political campaign fairly and squarely on my state roads bill, and ran two hundred votes ahead of my ticket. I intend to re-introduce my roads bill the first day of the session, and am more thoroughly in earnest to secure its passage than ever before. With political sentiment rapidly crystallizing in favor of the measure, the prospect is brighter than ever."

We heartily wish him the success he deserves.

In this connection it may properly be said that the Richardson bill is designed to be the most far reaching and immediate in its effects of all the state legislation thus far proposed on the roads question. It provides that the governor, with the consent of the senate, shall appoint four competent citizens of the state to be commissioners of state roads. These commissioners shall be divided equally between the two principal political parties, and when appointed shall be authorized to borrow, on the credit of the state, the sum of ten millions of dollars, at a rate of interest not exceeding three per cent. per annum, and reimbursable at such times as the commissioners may determine, not exceeding, however, the term of eighteen years from the date of the loan. Moneys raised on this loan are to be applied exclusively to the payment of cost of surveying, laying out, constructing and maintaining state roads in the several counties of the state; not, however, within the limits of any cities or incorporated villages. The location of these roads is to be decided by the state engineer, under direction of the commissioners, and under their approval the state engineer and surveyor is to determine the character and kind of roads to be constructed in the different localities. All work is to be done by contract, let to the lowest possible bidder, and the commissioners are at liberty to utilize, as far as practicable, the labor of convicts in the state prisons, penitentiaries and jails, as well as that of paupers and tramps who may be supported at the public expense. Turnpikes belonging to private corporations may be included in the line of improved state roads under this bill, and compensation is to be made to the proprietors, under agreement with the commissioners, or by condemnation proceedings and appraisal, in case an agreement cannot be reached. To become a law, this bill, by reason of its peculiar constitutional features, requires the approval of the people at a general election, and its passage by the legislature will therefore open the way to a widely interesting and lively issue in the State of New York upon the subject of better roads.

THE subject of free delivery of mails in the rural districts has been exploited with much prominence in the last report of the Postmaster General, and seems now to be engaging the attention of farmers in all parts of the country, and at the last session of the National Grange, at which thirty-three states were represented, the measure received unanimous approval. The current number of the *Farm Journal* publishes a very interesting article in support of the new scheme. We quote :

"Our last Congress appropriated $10,000 to make a preliminary test. Forty-six country post-offices in thirty states, and covering as many of the varied conditions of our great country as possible, were selected for the trial. Of these, all but seven at the end of several months showed an increase over former receipts and usual gain, of enough to pay the entire cost of the new service and leave a profit besides. Seven did not quite reach the cost. The increase of gross receipts in thirty-nine offices amounted to $6,213.49. Deducting what rightly belonged to natural increase, and the net balance to the credit of the free delivery service amounted to $850.50. This success is a wonderful showing when it is considered that in the establishment of the free delivery system the patrons of the office stopped paying box rent, and the loss on box rents was therefore taken from the gross receipts. The forty-six free delivery offices aggregated 285 months of free delivery service, at a total cost for carriers of $4,420.69, and a net profit, as before said of, $850.50. An entire year of these offices aggregating 552 months would, at the above rate, have resulted in a net earning of $3,812.54. and this *profit* is on an appropriation of only $10,000. With an appropriation of $200,000 for a year on these figures, for a basis of estimate, the net earnings, or profit to the Government, would reach $76,250.80. How many farmers are now paying $2 or more a year for a post-office box miles away from their farms? Based on the above figures of actual practice, for only twenty to forty cents *a year* for each inhabitant, the mail can be brought to each door. How many farmers would gladly give that in a hurried season to have their mail brought a single time? The cost of the extra carriers amounts to from $100 to $200 each per year. Unlike city carriers, those in the villages and in the country will not generally be required to give all their time. * *

Urge this just measure *now* upon your Congressmen and United States senators. Think about it ; talk about it ; work for it, and it will come. ' Heaven helps those who try to help themselves.' "

GEN. ROY STONE, whose active interest has made him prominent in the work for better roads since the beginning of the movement, has been recently at work on a plan for enlisting legislation by the general government for the improvement of roads throughout the country. A memorandum prepared by General Stone is before us. It includes the following features:

1. A National Highway Commission, to be composed of two senators, five members of the House of Representatives, and five citizens to be appointed by the President of the United States, together with the Secretaries of War and Interior, and the Postmaster General, who may be represented by subordinates from their respective departments, and also an associate member from each of the states and territories that may choose to appoint one. 2. The commission to continue for two years, and to hold its sessions in Washington during the sessions of Congress, in Chicago during the World's Fair, and elsewhere at other times. 3. Among the duties of the commission to be : (*a*) To formulate plans for a National School of Roads and Bridges, with provision for branches to be connected with the various agricultural colleges and experiment stations. (*b*) To collate the various recent state laws regarding highway improvement, with full information of their practical workings, and to suggest such a combination or modifications of the provisions of those laws, as may secure the best form of state aid to local communities in road construction. (*c*) To inquire into the practice of other countries, and report whether any form of national aid is desirable here and how it might be given. (*d*) To collect and disseminate general information regarding roads and their improvement, and especially to provide for the exhibition at the World's Fair of the best methods and appliances for road-making, with organized free instructions in the art to all who may desire it. (*e*) To consider and report whether, in any part of the United States, post or military roads could profitably be established and built by the government as examples in road construction.

Gen. Stone has laid his proposition before his co-workers, and has sent memorandum outline of the plan to prominent men in official positions, so that the entire matter may be well considered before being incorporated in a Congressional bill. The scheme is certainly an important and far-reaching one, and is well worth the attention of our national law makers.

THE property owners interested in the extension of St. Mary's Avenue, met at Rosebank (Staten Island) on the evening of December 15, and began formal proceedings to secure the extension of that avenue for a distance of about half a mile. All the property owners, with one exception, were represented at the meeting and approved the project. The rapid development of property values on Staten Island within the last few years, is largely, if not mainly due to the interest shown by the people of Richmond County in the improvement and extension of their streets and avenues.

———

THE Richmond, Virginia, *Times*, of December 13, is out with a strong editorial in favor of improved road laws for Virginia. The editor says: " The fact that a number of counties have obtained from the Legislature special road laws for themselves shows the effort to struggle from under the present system, which is conspicuous for its inefficiency in making good roads and the opportunity it affords for shiftlessness and fraud. * * * The general operation of our road laws is unbusinesslike and unfair. * * * They really produce but little good and tend to educate the people in the belief that the public service demands the least amount of activity and capacity, and that the public coffers are open to the plunder of conscienceless officers."

What is here stated of the existing road laws of Virginia might be truthfully repeated regarding similar laws in other States. It is beginning to be generally understood not only that the labor applied by Tom, Dick and Harry in the working out of their annual road tax is lazily, slovenly and uselessly applied; but that the moneys collected by the road officers in many of the States have too often gone into the pockets of the collectors instead of into the public coffers. In the face of this gigantic system of petty stealing, which the people have tolerated for a hundred years, because of its inconsiderable character in individual cases, it is difficult to hear with patience the moss-back objections to engineers and commissions upon the ground that commissions do not always handle public funds to the best advantage. Let us by all means have the money placed in the hands of responsible men, and have the plans of expenditure so systematized that we may all know what is done with the funds.

———

LIKE Oliver Twist, the good people of New Jersey want more. Not satisfied with the splendid development of traffic and property values which has followed the building of good roads in and about Union and Essex Counties, they have resolved upon a State Convention to be held at the State House, Trenton on January 22, 1892, at the conclusion of the annual session of the Board of Agriculture. The Executive Committee of this Board has been corresponding with prominent men in different parts of the State, and a formal call has been issued to secure a representative attendance at the Convention. The Governor is deeply interested in the scheme, and will probably make recommendations to the Legislature, looking to the development of legislation for good roads in all of the several counties. Secretary Dye of the State Board of Agriculture has the co-operation of Chief Consul G. Carlton Brown, of the New Jersey Division of the League of American Wheelmen, and the entire aid and influence of that Division will be exerted to support the project in question.

At the Convention a number of papers will be read. Thomas H. Dudley, of Camden, will, it is expected, read a paper on "European Roads." It is possible that the outcome of the Convention will be a commission to codify the present muddled road laws, and devise such legislation as will place roads under the supervision of the State and counties, and that a permanent commission will be created to designate State roads and look after them.

THE Carriage Builders' National Association, at its recent Cincinnati Convention, adopted the report of Colonel Albert A. Pope, as Chairman of the Committee on the Improvement of the Roads, and passed formal resolutions commending the work of Colonel Pope and recommending a special committee of two members from each State, to be selected by the Executive Committee, and authorized to urge upon the various State Legislatures the need of better road laws and appropriate legislation.

MISSOURI stands prominent among the Western States in her movement for improved roads. At a recent meeting of the State Board of Agriculture, at Fulton, special prominence was given to the subject of better country roads, and Hon. J. L. Erwin, of Fulton, was made President of a new State association designed to encourage this work. In view of a probable extra session of the Legislature during the present winter, a petition has been widely circulated through the State, asking Governor Francis to make special mention of the necessity of road legislation in issuing his official call for the special session. To Chief Consul. Holm, and his able co-workers in the Missouri Division, is due much credit for the active feeling now manifested in Missouri in favor of good roads.

THE following cheerful Christmas telegram was sent over the wires of the Associated Press from Burlington, Iowa :

"BURLINGTON, Iowa, December 25.— It would take a round $1,000,000 to even up the losses in trade to the merchants, shippers, and farmers in Iowa on account of the fearful mud blockade which exists, not only in Iowa, but all over the Mississippi Valley. For two weeks country roads in Iowa, Missouri and Illinois have been hub deep in mud, and the farming communities have been virtually padlocked on the farm. As a result, merchants depending on country trade have suffered immense financial loss, especially in holiday trade, while the farmers and shippers have lost by inability to market their products. It is feared many failures among country merchants may result."

Every farmer and merchant in the United States should be compelled by law to read that telegram three times a day for the next six months. If somebody had suggested last fall to the people of the Mississippi Valley that a million dollars of their money invested in the improvement of roads would be well spent, the suggestion would most likely have been laughed at, and if a law had been passed imposing upon the farmers and merchants of that section, a tax of one million dollars for roads improvement, a mental panic would have occurred, which, in noise, riot, and general disaster, would have resembled an earthquake. But the million has gone, and the roads are no better.

TENNESSEE is beginning to show a live interest in the good work. The Agricultural Experiment Station at Memphis recently issued a pamphlet containing valuable points on the improvement of country roads, and now an active movement has begun in Knox County, for the extension of the celebrated pikes in that section. A writer in the Knoxville *Journal* of December 28, says :

"Over ninety per cent. of the taxes of Knox County are collected within a radius of five miles from the custom house, and if the cheap lands of the remote districts are to enjoy the favor of good roads from a fund, 90 cents on the dollar of which is raised from this city and suburbs, a contribution of free hauling certainly appears fair enough, and in addition the great saving of time will be an ample reward.

"There is serious discussion on the part of some members of the county court, it is said, to build more than double the miles of pike in 1892 than was ever built in one year before."

———

THE illustrated pamphlets published by the Roads Improvement Department of the League of American Wheelmen during the last year have attracted the attention of foreign readers, and applications have been received from the proprietors of English and French publications for permission to reproduce the plates and printed matter in their columns.

———

THE Overman Wheel Company has published a most unique little vest pocket pamphlet on "Power of Wheels." It is all included within six pages containing only about 300 words, and a portion of it runs like this:

"Do you know that the wheel is the connecting link between barbarism and civilization, poverty and wealth; that by it the world moves, and upon it all great work depends? Do you know that the horse which staggers with 500 pounds upon his back trots off easily with 2,000 pounds loaded on wheels? Do you know that if you were chained to 500 pounds of iron in the form of a cube you would die if bread was but one-eighth of a mile off?— that in a cask you could roll 2,000 pounds around the earth? Do you know that every time you step you lift your weight (say 100 lbs.) one inch, which, added up, makes a lot at the end of a day?—that on a bicycle you can go farther, faster and easier in the same time? Take the wheel from the locomotive, and one-half the world's industry would die. Remove it from the car, carriage and factory and the wealth of the world would dwindle nine-tenths. You would hear of no Goulds, no Astors, no Vanderbilts. Wall Street would go down a tradition to future generations."

———

WE are indebted to Hon. Mortimer Whitehead, Official Lecturer of the National Grange, Patrons of Husbandry, for valuable printed matter relating to the affairs of that body, including a most interesting report on the "Rural Free Delivery of Mail." Mr. Whitehead writes us that the farmers in the Grange organizations have been discussing the question of good roads for some time, and that much good is coming out of it.

———

BY way of editorial novelty, the New York *Sun* has lately taken upon itself the interesting task of computing the probable population of Hell. It estimates as follows:

"In round numbers the earth has a population of 1,300,000,000, of whom 300,-000,000 are professed Christians, the other 1,000,000,000 being Mohammedans, Buddhists, Jews, pagans, and heathens. The whole race was condemned to eternal punishment for the sin of Adam. This was the fall of man, from which there was and is no redemption save through the death of Christ. Biblical chronology gives the earth a period about 6,000 years. From Adam's time to Christ was 4,000 years, during which period no human souls were saved. The population may then have averaged 1,000,000,000. Three generations, or 3,000,000,000, pass away in each century. Forty centuries, therefore, consigned 120,000,000,000 of men to eternal fire, and, for all we know, they are there now. In the 1,900 years that have elapsed since the birth of Christ, 57,000,000,000 more of human beings have lived and died. If all the Christians, nominal and real, who have ever lived on the face of the earth have been saved, they would not number more than 18,000,000,000. Now, if we deduct this latter number from the grand total of 177,000,000,000, we find 159,000,000,000 of souls who are suffering the torments of hell fire, as against the 18,000,000,000 who have escaped. But this is not the whole truth. Nobody believes that more than ten per cent. of the professed Christians are saved. Calvinists say that the elect are few. If this is a fact, Heaven contains but 1,800,000,000, against a population in Hell of 175,000,000,000."

We don't like to criticise the treatment of a subject with which we have so meagre an acquaintance; and it is enough for us to believe that mud roads will not be tolerated in Paradise, and that they will quickly dry up in the other place; but, without intending any piracy upon Mr. Dana's new field of speculation, we might suggest that his statistics indicate a tremendous field for the circulation of an asbestos newspaper.

BORROWED WIT

THE SPOONY MARRIED MAN.

'Tis mostly trifles in this world that make our sum of
woe,
A sort of moral insect tribe that stings where'er we go;
But of all plagues devised to mar the great terrestrial
plan,
I think the biggest nuisance is the spoony married
man,
With his
    "Petsie, itsie darling, place oo hand in mine,
      Round oo little dainty waist, arm um twinum
      twine ;
      Tiss oo huggen huzzens, while um smoove um
      turls,
      Don't be tross and fretful, now, oo baddest ittle
      dirls !"

A Jew once had an enemy who kept a big hotel,
Down where the waters green and cool in crested billows
swell;
He sought revenge, but much despised all common
modes of strife,
He simply sent as boarders there a spoony man and
wife,
It was
    "Itsie, bitsie wild bird, pining for its mate,
      Bad tunductor stopum train, make um husband late,
      Brought um's dess and bonbons, Cinderella's
      s'oos,
      Birdie nest on dear one's breast, while um tell um
      news."

Full soon the boarders left the stoop, and some came
home with jags,
Each morn revealed a jostling line of town-bound
traveling bags ;
They pleaded business, flood, and fire, shipwreck and
loss of life,
But no one breathed a word about the spoony man and
wife.

The landlord wildly paced the beach, and gazed upon
the surf,
He thought the money rashly spent, or dropped upon
the turf ;
"But what has ever brought me this?" he cried in wild
despair,
When suddenly be came upon this spoony married pair.
It was
    "Tootsie, wootsie dum-drop, ittle huzzens tum,
      Don't oo pout so naughty, don't oo bite oo thumb,
      Ownest tried to get here sooner than him am,
      Muzzer's bird of birdies and dear's one's pettest
      lamb."

The landlord raged and stamped and tore ; his passion
knew no bounds ;
He bade the man, with one wild roar, to quit his house
and grounds ;
He fired his baggage in the sand and chased him with a
knife,
And now contests a lawsuit with the spoony man and
wife.   —*George E. Detyr.*

"What are you opening that can of
tomatoes with ?" inquired a wife, gently,
from a room adjoining the kitchen.

"Why, with a can opener of course,"
growled the irate husband. "Did you
suppose I was opening it with my teeth ?"

"No," rejoined the wife, more gently
than before ; "but from the tenor of your
remarks I thought you might be opening
it with prayer."

I notice that in every jury there is at
least one crank. There was one juryman
who hung the jury for six hours because
the prisoner was deaf. He said he had
read somewhere that it was contrary to
the Constitution to convict a man without
a hearing, and he hoped that his right
arm might cleave to the roof of his mouth,
if he ever went back on the Constitution
of the United States.—*New York Herald.*

Peddler : "Beg pardon, ma'am, but I
am agent for Dr. Feeder's Spice Root Bit-
ters, and I'm sure if the members of your
family would try them they would soon
have the finest appetites."

Lady at Door (severely) : "This, sir, is
a boarding house."

Saidso : Since Jackson returned from
his Western trip he seems to have a mania
for damming Niagara.

Herdso : Sad case ; fell in with the hack-
men, I suppose.

If Little Babies
Could Write

WHAT a host of grateful letters the proprietors of the CUTICURA REMEDIES would receive. How their little hearts would overflow in ink. *They* know what they have suffered from itching and burning eczemas and other itching, scaly, blotchy, and pimply skin and scalp diseases before the **Cuticura Remedies** were applied. Parents, are you doing right by your little ones to delay a moment longer the use of these great skin cures, blood purifiers, and humor remedies?

Everything about the **Cuticura Remedies** invites the confidence of parents. They are absolutely pure, and may be used on the youngest infants. They are agreeable to the most sensitive. They afford instant relief in the severest forms of agonizing, itching, and burning skin and scalp diseases, and are by far the most economical (because so speedy) of all similar remedies. There can be no doubt that they daily perform more great cures than all other skin and blood remedies combined. Mothers and children are among their warmest friends. ☞ *Summer, when the pores open freely, is the best time to cure skin diseases.*

"ALL ABOUT THE SKIN" mailed free to any address, 64 pages, 300 Diseases, 50 Illustrations, 100 Testimonials. A book of priceless value to mothers, affording information not obtainable elsewhere.

CUTICURA REMEDIES are sold everywhere. Price, CUTICURA, the Great Skin Cure, 50c.; CUTICURA SOAP, an Exquisite Skin Purifier and Beautifier, 25c.; CUTICURA RESOLVENT, the greatest of Blood Purifiers and Humor Remedies, $1.00. Prepared by the POTTER DRUG AND CHEMICAL CORPORATION, BOSTON, MASS., U.S.A.

Pimples, Blackheads, red, rough, and oily skin and hands, and simple humors and blemishes of infants and children prevented and cured by that greatest of all Skin Purifiers and Beautifiers, the celebrated **Cuticura Soap.** For the prevention of tan, freckles, and sunburn, and for giving a brilliancy and freshness to the complexion, **Cuticura Soap** is incomparably superior to all so-called skin and complexion soaps. Sale greater than the combined sale of all other skin soaps.

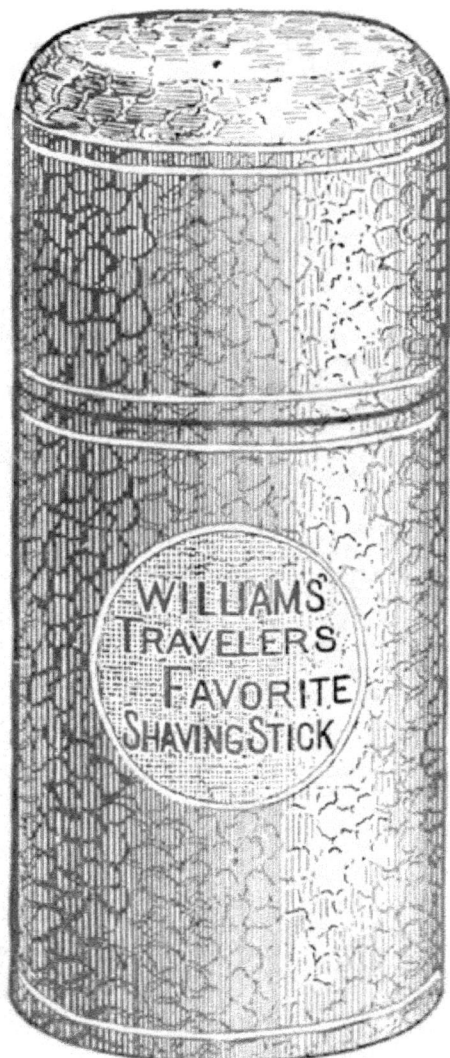

WILLIAMS'
TRAVELERS
FAVORITE
ShavingStick

Do You Shave Yourself?

—Then make a **Luxury** of the exercise. **WILLIAMS' SHAVING STICK** offers the means of doing so. Soft, delicate, cream-like lather! Exquisitely scented with the most delicate **ATTAR OF ROSES**. The new case is a beauty. Strong, durable. Never breaks, ends never come out. Travel a million miles with it—always intact. Rich maroon leatherette cover, good lacquered metal inside. Ask your Druggist for it **AT ONCE**. It cost no more than others.

☞ If your Druggist does not have WILLIAMS' SHAVING STICK, we will mail you one neatly packed, postage paid, for 25c. in stamps. One WILLIAMS' SHAVING STICK is enough for 250 shaves. 10 comfortable, refreshing shaves for ONE CENT. Try It.

Address **THE J. B. WILLIAMS CO.**, Glastonbury, Conn.,
Established half a hundred years. Makers of the famous GENUINE YANKEE SHAVING SOAP.

Baby-Skin

No fine lady or grown-up girl has a skin like a baby's—not quite.

All toilet soaps but Pears' have alkali in them probably.

Babies get washed with these soaps; their tender skins are made rough and red and sore; and yet the force of nature resists; there is no skin like the velvety baby-skin.

Have n't you seen a girl or woman catch sight of a dainty baby and break into smiles all over her face? and, if publicity does not forbid, you have seen her rush to the little stranger, seize his hands and toes, and go into raptures over the pink and softness!

That's the charm of baby-skin; not of the baby—nobody goes for a pimply baby.

Every woman whose place in the world permits, and every man (though men are not supposed to tell of it) wants, in proper measure, a baby-skin. Even the college athlete is not exempt.

Let them use Pears' Soap, which is nothing but soap; pure soap, which is nothing but Pears'.

We all have a baby-skin, unless it is eaten away by alkali. Soap will find it. Nothing but soap will find it. It may be well disguised—Pears' Soap will find it.

AND
...GOOD VEHICLES.

THE primary design of good roads is to make the best wheeling possible for every citizen.

Every citizen is entitled to travel over the highway in some sort of vehicle. To do this in the best manner he needs a good vehicle and a good road. A good vehicle first, because a good vehicle will get over a poor road. A poor vehicle on a good road is a poor thing at best, while a good vehicle on a good road is the climax.

In the foregoing pages you have been told how to make good roads. We wish to tell you how to get a good vehicle already made.

Several hundred thousand people in this country are using as a vehicle, on the roads, the bicycle. It has its recognized place, commercially and legally. It is used in the pursuit of business and pleasure. It demands the best of roads.

First in seniority of business and superiority of manufacture stand the

...COLUMBIA BICYCLES...

They are already well known, and their popularity is their strongest testimonial.

Our handsome new catalogue, the finest bicycle catalogue ever printed, gives full information in regard to them. Free on personal application to the nearest agent, or sent by mail on receipt of two 2-cent stamps.

POPE MFG. CO.
221 COLUMBUS AVENUE,
BOSTON, MASS.

12 WARREN ST., NEW YORK.
291 WABASH AVE., CHICAGO.

Factory:
HARTFORD, CONN.

www.ingramcontent.com/pod-product-compliance
Lightning Source LLC
Chambersburg PA
CBHW021535270326
41930CB00008B/1264